IF LIN CAN

How Jeremy Lin Inspired Asian Americans to Shoot for the Stars

Richard Ho

Illustrated by
Huỳnh Kim Liên and
Phùng Nguyên Quang

ini Charlesbridge

For Meir, Dovid, Ezra, and Binyamin.
You most definitely can.—R. H.

To my sister, Nguyen.—P. N. Q.

Published by Charlesbridge
9 Galen Street
Watertown, MA 02472
(617) 926-0329
www.charlesbridge.com

Printed in Malaysia
(hc) 10 9 8 7 6 5 4 3 2 1

Library of Congress Cataloging-in-Publication Data
Names: Ho, Richard (Children's author), author. | Phùng, Nguyên
    Quang, illustrator. | Huỳnh, Kim Liên, illustrator.
Title: If Lin Can: how Jeremy Lin inspired Asian Americans to shoot
    for the stars / Richard Ho; illustrated by Phùng Nguyên Quang
    and Huỳnh Kim Liên.
Description: Watertown, MA: Charlesbridge, [2024] | Includes
    bibliographical references. | Audience: Ages 7–10 years | Audience:
    Grades 2–3 | Summary: "This picture-book biography encourages
    children to look to the story of Jeremy Lin, the first NBA basketball
    player of Chinese or Taiwanese descent, for inspiration and
    empowerment."—Provided by publisher.
Identifiers: LCCN 2022058430 (print) | LCCN 2022058431 (ebook) |
    ISBN 9781623543723 (hardcover) | ISBN 9781632893536 (ebook)
Subjects: LCSH: Lin, Jeremy, 1988–Juvenile literature. | Basketball
    players–United States–Biography–Juvenile literature. | Asian
    American basketball players–United States–Biography–Juvenile
    literature. | National Basketball Association–History–Juvenile
    literature. | Asian American athletes–United States–Biography–
    Juvenile literature. | Discrimination in sports–Juvenile literature.
Classification: LCC GV884.L586 H6 2024 (print) | LCC GV884.L586
    (ebook) | DDC 796.323092 [B]–dc23/eng/20230627
LC record available at https://lccn.loc.gov/2022058430
LC ebook record available at https://lccn.loc.gov/2022058431

Illustrations done in digital media
Display type set in Buntaro by David Kerkhoff
Text type set in Brandon Grotesque and Mikado by
    Hannes von Döhren
Printed by Papercraft in Johor, Malaysia
Production supervision by Jennifer Most Delaney
Designed by Jon Simeon

Have you ever been told that you *can't*?

Can't climb that rope.

Can't star in the play.

Can't run for class president.

Have you ever been told what you're *not*?

Not athletic enough.

Don't look the part.

Don't ever speak up.

Have you ever felt underestimated?

Misunderstood?

Have you ever doubted
that you *can*?

You're not alone.

But . . .

Have you ever tuned in to a radio,

turned on a television,

or opened a newspaper,

Have you ever heard someone describe his challenges and felt like he was describing yours?

How people made fun of his size,

his race,

and his game.

How he practiced hard,

grew taller,

and kept his faith.

How he opened eyes everywhere he played

but still got passed over.

How he joined his hometown team

but couldn't get on the court.

How he moved to another team

and then another, but stayed glued to the bench.

How he slept on couches,

kept working,

and waited for
his chance.

How he refused to believe that he *couldn't*
and never doubted that he *could*.

How one night in February, in the world's most famous arena,

in the city that never sleeps,

he finally got his shot.

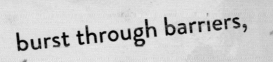

burst through barriers,

and made you feel proud of who you are?

Have you ever believed that
you could reach for the stars,

be a star,

or lead the world?

Now ask yourself:

IF LIN CAN, WHY CAN'T I?

JEREMY'S JOURNEY

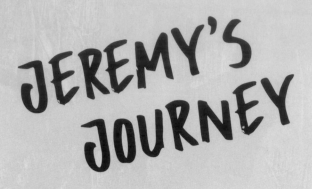

Jeremy Lin is famous around the world—from New York to Asia and everywhere in between. But at heart, he's a California kid.

Jeremy was born in Torrance, California, on August 23, 1988. He grew up in Palo Alto, a city in the Bay Area near San Francisco. His parents emigrated from Taiwan to the United States in the 1970s.

As a kid, Jeremy spent countless hours playing basketball at the local YMCA with his brothers, Josh and Joseph. In his senior year, Jeremy led an underdog Palo Alto High School team to a surprise state championship over a nationally ranked opponent. Despite a successful high school career, though, he received no scholarship offers from top basketball colleges.

So Jeremy chose to attend Harvard University instead. The prestigious school is known more for academics than sports, but Jeremy worked hard to prove himself as a basketball player. Over the next four years, he established himself as a dynamic point guard and one of the best players in Harvard's history. In the process, he opened a lot of eyes to the possibility of an Asian basketball star! Asian players had long been stereotyped as being too short or unathletic to excel at the sport. Jeremy's success on the court earned the respect of many fans and experts.

Even then, doubts remained about Jeremy's ability to make it as a professional basketball player. Outplaying other college players was one thing—but could he do it against the best players in the world? He entered the 2010 NBA draft, hoping one of the league's thirty teams would pick him. No team did—but Jeremy didn't give up! To show off his skills, he participated in the NBA's Summer League tournament, where he played well enough to receive offers from several teams. He signed a contract with his hometown Golden State Warriors for the 2010–2011 season.

Jeremy's signing was celebrated by Asian Americans around the country, especially the large Asian American population of the Bay Area. He made history in his first game, when he became the first American of Chinese or Taiwanese descent to play in the NBA. Unfortunately, he didn't get much playing time during his first season. The Warriors cut Jeremy

from the team before the following season, and he briefly joined the Houston Rockets before he was waived again. Running low on options, he signed with the New York Knicks early in the 2011–2012 season.

At first, Jeremy had trouble getting on the court with the Knicks. But injuries to veteran players and the team's long losing streak resulted in a golden opportunity for him. On February 4, 2012, Jeremy scored twenty-five points with seven assists and five rebounds in a win against the New Jersey Nets. The Knicks went on to win the next six games in a row, led by Jeremy's stellar play. He became the first player in NBA history to score at least twenty points and have at least seven assists in each of his first five starts. Every game brought more highlights, and media coverage exploded! Jeremy was everywhere, on TV and in newspapers and magazines. In just a few weeks, he became a global superstar. The excitement surrounding his rise was dubbed "Linsanity."

Given Jeremy's popularity and skills, a long career with the Knicks seemed like a sure thing. But due to difficult contract negotiations, he returned to the Houston Rockets the following season. Unfortunately, a series of injuries kept him off the court for long stretches of time. He went on to play for several more teams over the next eight seasons, including the 2019 NBA Champion Toronto Raptors. He was the first Asian American to win an NBA championship.

In the summer of 2019, Jeremy signed a contract to play for the Beijing Ducks of the Chinese Basketball Association. He has played several seasons in China and Taiwan, and his passion for the game remains strong.

A lifelong devout Christian and longtime advocate for Asian American rights, Jeremy has donated millions of dollars to charitable organizations and has spoken out against the rise of anti-Asian racism during the COVID-19 pandemic. He also devotes time to the Jeremy Lin Foundation, with the mission of empowering underrepresented youth throughout the country. In 2021, he was named a UNICEF Ambassador, a role that allows him to speak about the importance of mental health for children around the world.

As someone who struggled with anxiety, self-doubt, and racism throughout his playing career, Jeremy hopes his experience can benefit kids who are going through similar challenges. "What I would really love to see conveyed to the next generation is this belief of confidence," said Jeremy in an interview with NBC Asian America, "and having a deep confidence and security in who you are, and not being ashamed of that."

AUTHOR'S NOTE

Linsanity was a gift just for me.

At least that's how it felt at the time. Prior to Jeremy Lin's astronomical rise, I had never witnessed a star athlete who reflected so many aspects of my identity. Chinese American. Harvard graduate. And he played for the Knicks, the team I grew up rooting for with my basketball-loving father. For the first time, the sports world—and the world beyond sports—was captivated by someone like me. (That is, if I was six inches taller and eighty pounds heavier and had world-class basketball skills.)

For a magical two-week stretch in 2012, Jeremy gave Asian Americans a sports hero who reflected our experiences. As he dazzled us with crossover dribbles, pinpoint passes, and buzzer-beating threes, he also talked about being overlooked, overcoming racial stereotypes, and proving skeptics wrong. His struggles were our struggles, so his triumphs were our triumphs. He made us believe that if he could succeed, so could we.

That's why I tuned in to watch this slim Asian point guard light up the court at Madison Square Garden, going shot for shot with superstars like Kobe Bryant. That's why I called up my father after every game to breathlessly discuss the latest feats of our new favorite Knick. Because every high-five Jeremy got from a teammate was like a high-five to the five-year-old I used to be—the kid who had a Patrick Ewing poster on his wall but would have loved to have a Jeremy Lin poster next to it.

My only regret is that I was already an adult when Linsanity happened. How powerful would it have been for me as a child? I'm sure that the magic of the moment transformed many dreamers into believers, and that many of those kids who cheered for Jeremy then are busy changing the world today.

Linsanity inspired an entire generation of young people to say, "I can." I can only hope this book does the same.

SELECTED BIBLIOGRAPHY

BOOKS

Dalrymple, Timothy. *Jeremy Lin: The Reason for the Linsanity*. New York: Center Street, 2012.

Yorkey, Mike. *Linspired: The Remarkable Rise of Jeremy Lin*. Grand Rapids, MI: Zondervan, 2012.

WEBSITES

The official website of Jeremy Lin: www.jlin7.com

Jeremy Lin Foundation: www.jeremylinfoundation.org

Basketball Reference, Jeremy Lin: www.basketball-reference.com/players/l/linje01.html

VIDEOS

The Aspen Institute. "Conversation with Jeremy Lin: Mental Health and Racial Bias in Youth Sports." YouTube video, 20:39. October 19, 2021. www.youtube.com/watch?v=Ni2KzDZ_PcE

Chi, Frank. *38 at the Garden*. Documentary on Max, 38:00. 2022. www.hbo.com/movies/38-at-the-garden